GW01454213

CORN RECIPES FROM THE INDIANS

Compiled by
Frances Gwaltney

With an Introduction
by
Mary Ulmer Chiltoskey

Copyright 1988 Frances Gwaltney

Published by
CHEROKEE PUBLICATIONS
P.O. BOX 256
CHEROKEE, NC 28719

THE LEGEND OF CORN

The ancient ones in time of need
Discovered how to use their seed,
The hunters threw aside their bows,
And planted corn in hills and rows.

The blood drenched corn of sacrifice;
The golden song which echoes thrice,
All bow down to the great sun God,
His high priest blesses, smiles and nods.

The Spanish conquerors of old
Took home this seed, instead of gold,
To plant it in the old, old soil,
To bring new life to those who toil.

Today the grain is used for feed,
And mills refine the golden seed;
Over the world the tall corn grows,
The gift of the Indian - the tall green rows.

By Dawn
Great, great granddaughter of
Sioux Chieftain, War Eagle.

CONTENTS

page

"The Legend of Corn", poem...2

Introduction...4

Foreword..5

Drinks 6

Desserts and snacks 9

Soup 12

Dumplings 15

Mush..16

Side Dishes..17

Meat and Corn 19

Bread 21

Miscellaneous 29

"How To's" 31

INTRODUCTION

When the Great One created the Indian (The Last of the five races), he soon had a need for curing this man of boredom. The Great One gave Man a companion. He created the first stalk of corn with Woman emerging from the top of the stalk. Woman accepted the corn as a token of her "roots", planting it in her yard until Turkey showed her that is was good for food.

When Columbus came to America he found the tropical and temperate zone Indians growing and using six kinds of corn. We have and use five of these now. Pod corn seems to have been lost, but sweet corn, popcorn, flour corn, flint corn and dent corn are still important crops. Corn is probably responsible for creating more wealth than all the gold found by the early explorers.

This book gives an excellent overview of how women through the ages have used corn to feed their families with the plant that is still sacred to the American Indians.

Mary Ulmer Chiltoskey
Cherokee, North Carolina

FORWARD

This book was inspired by Dr. H.F. Robinson, Chancellor Emeritus of Western Carolina University at Cullowhee, North Carolina. Dr. Robinson has been interested in the old native varieties of corn and their uses for many years, and is actively working on the improvement of the Cherokee flour corn.

Recipes in this book have two things in common; they all use corn, that most important and ubiquitous of Indian food, in one form or another, and every recipe is genuinely Indian.

Many recipes are dated, giving the year when the recipe was first collected in modern times, as far as I know. The donors of some recipes are quite illustrious. When any information is given about a person, it follows the first recipe attributed to that person.

Frances Gwaltney

DRINKS

ABUSKEE

Use roasting ears just before hardening. Break a grain to see if kernel is moist. Gather as much corn as you desire to parch. Shell corn, in large pan. Sift 1 1/2 gallons dry wood ashes into large iron kettle. Build a fire of medium heat, place kettle over it tilted at a 45 degree angle. Pour corn into the ashes and stir continually with wooden paddle until corn is brown. Remove corn and ashes, sift ashes from corn and put ashes back into pot. Continue process until all corn is parched. Pound or grind corn into fine meal. Take 2 heaping teaspoons to one glass of water, sweeten to taste, and you will have the delicious Creek Indian drink, "Abuskee".*
*Also see Parched Corn recipe, p. 30.

1955, Acee Blue Eagle, (famous Indian artist,)
As used by his grandmother.

OLD FIELD APRICOT DRINK Oo-Wa-Ga

Hull out the seeds and pulp of old field apricots, * put these on to boil with a tiny bit of soda to make the seeds separate from the pulp. Strain out the juice, add meal to the juice and cook until the meal is done.
*Passion Flower Fruit, Passiflora incarnata

1950 Aggie Ross Lossiah (Cherokee, N.C.)
Mrs. Lossiah's grandfather was John Ross, Principal Chief of the
Cherokee Nation at the time of the Removal in the 1830's.

COLD FLOUR (Drink)

Use roasting ears just before hardening, break a grain to see if the kernel is moist. Place the whole grains in a large kettle with wood ashes over a medium heat, stir continually until brown. Sift or separate from the ashes, pound or grind into fine meal. Take 2 tablespoons to a glass of water, sweeten to taste.

1932, Lilah D. Lindsey (Creek)

OSAFKEE, A DRINK

Combine 5 gallons of water, 3 quarts of hominy grits (either ground or pounded) and 1 pint of ash lye. Cook 3 hours. Hickory nut kernels may be added which makes a delicious flavor (if used, the lye should be omitted).

1932, Lilah D. Lindsey (Creek)

CAW -WHEE-SA-KA, A DRINK

Take flour corn, brown in oven until it will crumble, then pound into a flour, mix with water for a healthful drink. The old Indians always drank plenty when going on a long journey, hunting or fishing trip.

1932, Carrie Breedlove (Oklahoma Cherokee)

COFFEE

Parched corn was used for coffee.

1932, Lena Barnard (Piankashaw)

POZOLE

Mix fine cornmeal with water to make a dough. Shape into dough-balls about the size of a walnut. TO USE: Dissolve a dough-ball into water and drink.

Ancient Mayan. TODAY: Isolated Central American tribes.

GA-NO-HE-NA

Shell 5 or 6 ears of good hickory cane corn. Cover with lye made from ashes until the corn turns a golden yellow and its skin loosens off by pounding in a mortar. It is then pounded and riddled and whole grains put back and pounded until all are cracked. The husks are fanned out and put aside. The grits are boiled until done, and the husks, which always have lots of fine meal mixed with them from the pounding, should be washed out well, putting the water into the grits for a thickening. This much will make a small wash kettle full, to eat and drink.

1932, Bess Schrimsher Lewis (Oklahoma Cherokee)

HOMINY CORN DRINK

Shell corn and soak in Lye until the skin can be removed. Beat the corn until it is the size of hominy. Sift out the meal and cook the corn particles until done, adding a little meal to thicken. Drink hot or wait until it sours and drink it cold. The drink may be kept for quite a while unless the weather is very hot. It was customary to serve this drink to visiting friends.

1950, Mrs. Clifford Hornbuckle (Cherokee, N.C.)

BOTA CUPPOSA (Oklahoma Cherokee)

Parch dried corn, beat into flour. Put 2 tablespoons of the flour into a glass, add water and sugar. A traditional drink.

1955, Mr. and Mrs. William (Bill) Short(Chickasaw).
Mr.Short was president in 1953 of the
National Congress of American Indians.

HOMINY SOUP

Put hominy corn in Lye until the skin slips. Beat the corn, then sift the meal to remove the larger particles. Cook these larger pieces in water until done. Store this soup in a pottery jar and it will sour by the next day like buttermilk and may be kept 4 days before discarding. This drink was always served to visitors and was enjoyed by those working in the fields.

1950, Mollie Runningwolfe Sequoyah (Cherokee, N.C.)

DESSERTS AND SNACKS

AH-GEE-CHUM-BUH-GEE
1 lb. dried fruit
2 tablespoons brown sugar
2 cups corn meal, well sifted
    Cook fruit about half done in water that is 1 1/2" over the fruit. Pour scalding hot fruit over meal, soup and all. If meal is not soft enough to hold it's shape with the fruit and soup, add boiling water. Mold into round oblongs and wrap in corn shucks longwise, tie each end and two or three sections in the middle, drop into boiling water and cook covered until done. These were made especially for Indian children to be eaten between meals, like candy or cookies.

1955, Acee Blue Eagle (Creek)

HUCKLEBERRY DUMPLINGS
Boil huckleberries. Take berries out, leaving soup. Then use corn meal and flour as in making bread. Use baking powder to make rise. Roll flat, then drop into the huckleberry soup and cook until dumplings are done.

1932, Mrs. S.R. Lewis (Oklahoma Cherokee)

PEACH BREAD
Use soft free-stone peaches, mash together with meal about half and half, add small amount of sugar. If there isn't enough juice in peaches to make soft-hard dough, add boiling water.   Bake in pones.

1932, Bess Schrimsher Lewis (Oklahoma Cherokee)

BUFPO (Oklahoma Cherokee)
Parch peanuts and beat them into a fine meal, add1/3 as much Bota Cupposa (See recipe pg. 8) as peanut meal, mold like butter and slice.

1955, Mr. & Mrs. William Short (Chickasaws)

SIMI CHUMBO

1 pint sweet milk
2 tablespoons sugar
3 large tablespoons corn meal
1 cup hickory nuts, chopped fine

1/4 teaspoon salt
3 eggs
Lump of butter

Bring the milk to a boil, add meal, sugar, butter and salt and cook slowly until it thickens. Remove from heat, cool, and add the well beaten egg. Put in a baking dish and bake for 30 minutes in a moderate oven.

1955, Acee Blue Eagle (Creek)

INDIAN PUDDING

1 quart milk
1/4 cup water
1/2 cup molasses
1 egg, beaten
2 tablespoons sugar
1/2 teaspoon salt

1/2 cup stone-ground cornmeal
1/4 teaspoon each of nutmeg, ginger, cinnamon
1 tablespoon butter

Scald the milk. Mix the water, molasses and cornmeal and blend into milk and boil. Remove from heat and add butter, sugar and seasonings. Cool a little and add egg. Bake 1 hour at 325 degrees in a baking dish.

1972

INDIAN CAKE

4 cups sifted cornmeal
3 tablespoons molasses
Rounded tablespoon of lard or butter
2 teaspoons salt

Mix ingredients and add boiling water until mixture is well moistened. Put into a well-greased baking pan, smooth surface and bake in a hot oven until well browned.

1972

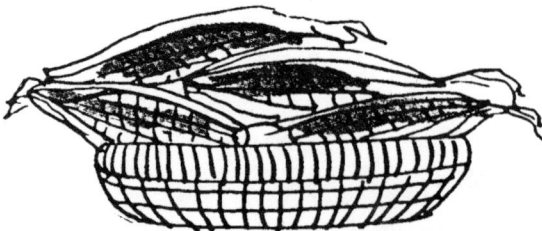

WECEMIZE WESNE

4 cups parched corn, ground fine
1 cup suet
2 cups dried wild choke cherries
Mix well together, let stand until firm, and slice for use as dessert.

1955, John Gates (Sioux)
(Mr. Gates' grandfather was
Chief Two-Bear of the Sioux Indians.)

SQUAW BREAD

2 tablespoons Royal baking powder, 1 quart luke warm water,
1 teaspoon salt, 1 tablespoon compound (Shortening) flour enough to
make about like bisquit dough. Roll and cut any shape desired. Fry in
kettle of boiling compound.

1932, Nancy Rogers Ware (Oklahoma Cherokee)

SYRUP FOR SQUAW BREAD

1 quart white corn syrup, 15¢ worth of brown sugar. Boil together, using
no water. Add 1 tablespoon of maple flavor. Take from fire and beat
1/2 cup bacon fryings into above ingredients.

1932, Nancy Rogers Ware (Oklahoma Cherokee)

INDIAN PUDDING

3 cups of sweet milk, meal to make it thick like mush, 1 cup shortening,
1 cup sugar, 1 cup raisins, 1 teaspoon salt, 1 teaspoon vanilla. Let the
milk come just to a boil and add the meal, then rest and bake in a slow
oven for 45 minutes.

1932, Margaret Jones Farris (Oklahoma Cherokee)

FRESH CORN PUDDING

2 cups fresh corn kernels   1 tablespoon sugar
3 eggs, beaten   pepper and nutmeg
4 tablespoons flour   2 Tbs. melted butter
1 teaspoon salt   2 cups milk

Mix all ingredients. Bake in a casserole dish set in a pan of water in a
325 degree oven for one hour or until pudding is firm.

1972

SOUPS

VEGETABLE SOUP - Canutchee

This is a combination of hickory nuts, hominy and sometimes sweet potatoes. Prepared by beating hickory nuts, and then with water shape into balls about the size of a baseball. After this has been done, at any time, take one ball or more and put in a pan of hot water and strain through sifter to separate the hulls. Then boil with hominy. Add sweet potatoes if desired and serve.

1932, Mrs. S.R. Lewis (Oklahoma Cherokee)

HOMINY SOUP

This soup is made from hominy, first by beating into grits, and then boil until tender. It is then ready to serve.

1932 Jane Ann Thompson Phillips (Oklahoma Cherokee)

CORNBREAD SOUP Se-Lu-Ga-Du Oo-Ga-Ma

Slice cold cornbread as thinly as possible. Toast both sides before the fire, drop into boiling water and season with grease and meat if available.

William Crowe and Goingback Chiltoskey (Cherokee, N.C.)
(Mr. Chiltoskey is a famous Cherokee Woodcarver.)
1950

MEAT SKIN SOUP

Boil any kind of meatskins until they are done, then bake or roast until brown. Put in water with a little salt and boil until it has a good flavor. Thicken with cornmeal and cook until the meal is done.

1950 William Crowe and Goingback Chiltoskey (Cherokee, N.C.)

SOFFKEE (SOFKEY)

For every six cups of water add one cup of coarse grits and cook in an iron pot until it has a milky look. Serve hot, dipping from the pot with large wooden spoons which can be bought in any Seminole village. This is almost a drink with chewy lumps of grits in it.

1967 (Seminole)

BEEF SOUP

Take sofkey grits, hominy and large chunks of beef, about 1 pound each, and boil together.

1932, Lilah D. Lindsey (Creek)

CORN CHOWDER

2 cups corn kernels
2 onions, chopped
2 tablespoons butter
salt and pepper

3 1/2 cups cubed potatoes
2 cups boiling water
3 1/2 cups scalded milk
1 slice salt pork, diced

Fry pork until done. Add onion and cook until transparent. Add potatoes and water and cook until potatoes are soft. Add corn, milk, butter and seasonings. Heat but do not boil.

1972

CORNMEAL GRAVY

Put some water (milk if you have it), salt and red pepper in a skillet where meat has been cooked, if you have meat, but if you don't have meat just put it in a clean skillet. Add cornmeal and cook until the meal is done. Eat this by itself or with bread for breakfast or with vegetables if you have some.

1950, Jim Will (Cherokee, North Carolina)

TA-FULLA (Choctaw)

To 1 quart of hominy add 1 gallon of water and 1/4 cake of bean ashes.*
Cook until corn is tender.
*See recipe for Bean Ash Cakes pg. 32

1955, Mr. & Mrs. William Short (Chickasaw)

HOMINY SOUP
1/4 lb. salt pork, sliced 1/4" thick
1 quart hominy
1 quart buttermilk
1 medium onion
1/4 teaspoon pepper
Render the salt pork in a large heavy kettle, then drain off grease. Slice onion thinly, add to pot and cook slowly until transparent. Mix in the hominy and heat about 5 minutes. Serve warm.

1976

SQUASH SOUP
1 Crookneck squash
3 cups dried corn
1/2 lb. salt pork, sliced
10 medium potatoes
Boil the salt pork for 1/2 hour. Add cut up squash and potatoes. Add corn wiich has been soaked and cooked. Cook until potatoes are tender. Season to taste.

1976

DRIED CORN SOUP
1 ear dried corn
7 cups water
1 strip fatback, sliced
5 oz. dried beef
1/8 teaspoon pepper
Pour boiling water (2 cups) over dried corn and cover. Let soak 2 or 3 hours. Place corn and water in a pot, add remaining water and the fatback and simmer for 3 hours or until corn is tender but not soft. Mix in the dried beef and pepper and simmer, stirring, for 10 minutes more.

1976

DUMPLINGS

FLAT DUMPLINGS
Make dumplings rather thin out of beaten meal and boil in water until done. After cooling, split open and spread in a flat basket. This basket was passed over the flame four times, once to the North, East, South and West, to keep the Skillies* away. Then the basket was set outside to freeze, to be eaten in the morning while still frozen. The smoke gave a very pleasant flavor to the bread, and old people especially enjoyed sitting by a good fire on a cold day, telling the young ones stories of the past while munching on a bit of frozen bread.

1950, Aggie Ross Lossiah (Cherokee, N.C.)

*Booger, Witch, Ghost, etc.

INDIAN DUMPLINGS WITH SEQUOYAH SAUCE
3 cups of meal, teaspoon of salt, 1/2 cup of ash lye (or 1 teaspoon soda). Mix well, pour boiling water over mixture to make a stiff dough, make into balls the size of Indian biscuits and drop into 2 quarts of boiling salted water. Cook 15 minutes. Take 3 tablespoons of dumpling dough, thin to a creamy thickness and pour into pot and cook 5 minutes longer.

1932, Mrs. Victoria Martin Rogers (Oklahoma Cherokee)

CORNMEAL DUMPLINGS
Make a preparation from corn meal as in making biscuits and drop into hot water, cooking slowly until done. Brown or pinto beans may be added. Serve hot.

1932, Mrs. S. R. Lewis (Oklahoma Cherokee)

BEAN DUMPLINGS
1 quart of meal, 2 cups of brown beans and 1/2 teaspoon of salt. Mix with boiling water, roll into small balls and drop into boiling water. Cook slowly until well done.

1932, Nannie Shelton Peebles (Oklahoma Cherokee)

LYE DUMPLINGS

Sift about 4 cups meal with 1 teaspoon soda and 1 teaspoon salt. Stir in boiling water until dough will hold it's shape when molded. Cook covered in boiling water until done. Soda turns the meal yellow like lye. Can be served with fried or boiled pork.

1955, Mrs. & Mrs. Watie Pettit (Okla. Cherokee)
Mr. Pettit was the former editor of the
New Cherokee Advocate, Tahlequah, Oklahoma.

BLUE DUMPLINGS

Scald whole white corn in lye water, drain until dry, pound into meal. Burn pea hulls* (black-eyed or cow-pea, or any kind) and pound to a powder, sift and add to your cornmeal; using hot water, knead into balls a size of a baseball, drop into boiling water and cook 1/2 hour. To one part of meal use 1/2 part of pea meal.
*See Bean Ash Cake recipe, p. 32.

1932, Lilah D. Lindsey (Creek)

MUSH

FISH AND MUSH

Barbeque fish on a stick, then cut into small pieces and boil in water to make a thick soup. Make mush by cooking cornmeal in water with a little lye or soda, then eat mush with the fish soup. This dish was always served to sick people when fish were available.

1950, Mrs. Katie Taylor Brady (Cherokee, N.C.)

MUSH A-Ni-S-Ta

While plain water comes to a boil in a pot, wet meal with a little cold water. Add the wet meal slowly to the boiling water and stir until done.

1950, Mollie Runningwolfe Sequoyah (Cherokee, N. C.)

MUSH A-NI-S-TA

Boil a pot of salted water, add cornmeal and cook until the meal is done. Serve with meat, soup or stew or alone.

1950, Mrs. Clifford Hornbuckle (Cherokee, N.C.)

SIDE DISHES

CORN AND BEANS

To skin corn take hot wood ashes, put together with corn in iron pot over fire, pour water over mixture and stir to crack the skin. When the skin has cracked, pour more water over the corn to cool it, mash it very thoroughly through several waters to remove the lye. Rub off the skin. When the corn is clean, put in pot and cover with water and cook until about half done. Add the beans and cook until both are tender. Serve hot or cold, or fry in grease to serve. Beaten walnut halves added to this and served with sugar or salt is a fine combination. Corn may be completely cooked and used by itself also.

1955, Watie Pettit (Oklahoma Cherokee)

FRIED CORN AND BEANS Se-Lu- A-Su-Yi- Tu-Yu

Skin flour corn with lye, then cook. Cook colored beans. Put the cooked corn and beans together and cook some more. (You may add pumpkin but be sure to cook until the pumpkin is done). Also add a mixture of cornmeal, beaten walnuts and hickory nuts and molasses to sweeten. Cook in an iron pot until the meal is done. May be eaten fresh or after it begins to sour. It will not keep after souring unless the weather is cold.

1950, Mrs. Clifford Hornbuckle (Cherokee, N.C.)

FRIED CORN AND BEANS

Cook skinned corn and colored beans separately, then put together and cook some more. Add a little grease and set aside to cool. When firm, slice and fry in hot grease.

1950, Mrs. Clifford Hornbuckle (Cherokee, N.C.)

FRIED CORN AND BEANS

Cook skinned corn and colored beans separately, then put together and cook some more. Add a little grease and set aside to cool. When firm, slice and fry in hot grease.

1950, Mrs. Clifford Hornbuckle (Cherokee, N.C.)

INDIAN DISH

1 cup of dried corn, 1 cup of pumpkin (dried or canned), salt and season with pork or meat fryings and add a little sugar, if you like.

1932, Rozelle Chouteau Lane (Osage)

SHAWNEE RECIPE FOR CORN

To a cob of corn, put enough water to steam thoroughly; mix with bacon grease. Fry in a skillet. This is especially good served with turkey or wild meats.

1932, Roberta Campbell Lawson (Delaware)

SUCCOTASH

2 cups green beans, shelled   2 tablespoons butter
2 cups new green corn, cut from cob   salt and pepper

Cover beans with water and simmer with salt until tender, then drain. Heat the corn then add to the beans. Season to taste and add butter. Bring to a boil and remove from fire at once.
Indians often added bits of meat or wild onions and peppers.

SUCCOTASH I-Ya-Tsu-Ya-Di-Su-Yi Se-Lu

Shell, then skin corn with lye. Cook corn and beans separately, then together. If desired, add pieces of pumpkin in time to get done.

1950, Agnes Catolster (Cherokee, N.C.)

MEAT AND CORN

DAKOTA WESHUNGLE

2 cups Indian sweet corn | 1 cup turnips*
3 lbs. fresh short ribs | 4 dried cow hoofs
2 cups dried pumpkin | 2 teaspoons salt
1 teaspoon black pepper

Cook cow hoofs over slow fire about 4 1/2 hours. Add other ingredients about 2 hours before serving.
*use wild prairie turnips if available.

1955, Mr. & Mrs. John Gates (Sioux)

CHICKEN AND CORN Tai-Ta-Gae A-Su-Yi Se-Lu

Stew chicken until done; add cooked, skinned corn. Cook together long enough to get a good flavor. Beans may be added if desired. Season with salt and pepper.

1950, Mrs. Clifford Hornbuckle (Cherokee, N.C.)

CHICKEN STEW

Cut a frying chicken in pieces, then brown in a deep pan. Cover with water and simmer one hour. Add 1/2 cup corn kernels, 1/2 cup of potatoes, 1/2 cup tomatoes, 1/4 cup onions and 1/2 cup limas or other shelled beans. Cook 20 minutes longer. Remove chicken and take meat from bones. Return meat to stew, reheat and serve. May be seasoned with salt, pepper and herbs.

1976

SCRAPPLE

Cook a fresh hog head until very tender. When the meat is cool, mince very fine and season. Then make a corn mush and as it cools, add the meat and then mold. Slice and dip in egg and fry to serve.

1932, Elizabeth Williams Audrain (Shawnee)

PASHOFA

Cook one gallon of corn half done, add 1/2 gallon pork chopped into small pieces and cook together until done. Salt to taste and add a dash of red pepper.

1955, Mr. & Mrs. William Short (Chickasaw)

TONSHLA BONA

Make a stew of fresh pork bones or fresh spare ribs or chicken. Cook hominy grits or prepared Tanfula until tender. Add no lye or soda. When the meat and Tanfula are both done combine and cook until the meat has seasoned the Tanfula. Though the Choctaws used no salt, the dish should be salted to taste for use today.

1955, Mrs. Green McCurtain (Choctaw)
(Mrs. McCurtain was the wife of Governor Green
McCurtain, last elected Governor of the Choctaw tribe.)

PIG'S FEET AND HOMINY

Cook 12 fresh pigs' feet until meat falls off the bone. When half cooked add 1 gallon of hominy and 2 dried red peppers and cookdown until it thickens. Salt to taste.

1955, Watie Pettit (Oklahoma Cherokee)

SOCK-KO-NIP-KEE

Prepare one squirrel, place in pot, cover with water and cook until tender. Add 4 cups sofkey grits (see pg. 13), cook together until consistency is like hominy. Rice is sometimes used in place of sofkey grits.

1955, Acee Blue Eagle (Creek)

CORN STEW

Many Indians made stews using wild onion and herbs for flavoring. The Sioux and other Plains Indians stewed buffalo, deer and other meat with potatoes and corn. The fresh corn was cut from the cob and added to the stew about 15 minutes before serving. Coastal Indians made stews of seafood and corn.

BREAD

KA NO NA
(Corn Beater)

MORTAR AND PESTLE

Where the words pound or grind are used, the best method is to use the mortar and pestle for pounding corn.

The mortar was a short log about three feet long, one end of which was hollowed out like a bowl about one foot deep to hold the shelled corn.

The pestle was longer. It was about two inches in diameter at one end and about six inches at the other.

Using the small end to fit into the opening of the log, the corn was pounded into meal.

BEAN BREAD

Take about 1 quart of corn meal which has been pounded in an old fashioned Indian mortar, or better, when the corn is nearly hard, grated on a large grater. Use corn field beans; boil 1 pint in plenty of water until tender; add teaspoon of salt, then pour over the meal, stirring all the time. Make a stiff dough, mix the beans in and bake in an old oven or skillet. Sweet potato bread is made the same way.

1932, Carrie Breedlove (Oklahoma Cherokee)

21

SOUR CORN BREAD

Take 1 gallon of sofkey grits (see pg. 13), soak overnight, next morning drip dry in a riddle or sugar sack. Pound or grind into meal; mix as for corn bread with salt, soda, baking powder, and 1 cup of flour; pour in a jar; set in a warm place to ferment for 12 hours, then pour into hot greased iron kettle and bake same as corn bread.

1932, Lilah D. Lindsey (Creek)

BEAN BREAD

1 cup of brown beans boiled until tender; drain in collander and cool. 2 cups of white cornmeal, 1 teaspoon salt, 1 tablespoon of lard, enough boiling water to make a stiff dough and beat well, fold in beans carefully; make into pones and bake 30 minutes.

1932, Victoria Martin Rogers (Oklahoma Cherokee)

BEAN BREAD

1 cup of pinto or chili beans; cook until tender, with 1 teaspoon of salt and seasoning. Take the soup and scald 3 cups of meal; have the dough stiff enough to make into pones with your hands, place in a dutch oven with hot coals on the lid, serve with plenty of butter.

1932, Anna Ballard Conner (Oklahoma Cherokee)

BROAD SOARDS

The same meal and bean mixture as the bean bread is fine wrapped in roasting ear shucks and roasted in hot ashes; fine when camping.

1932, Mr. Carrie Breedlove (Oklahoma Cherokee)

BEAN BREAD

Cook colored beans until done. Sift quart of meal. Use 1 pint of the beans and enough of its liquor (boiling hot) on meal, enough to make soft-stiff dough. Use hands and make into pones (about two), and bake brown in hot oven.

1932, Bess Schrimsher Lewis (Oklahoma Cherokee)

DOG HEADS
Grate corn before it is too hard and make a soft mixture.   Pat into cakes, wrap in green corn blades and boil 30 minutes. The Indians used very little salt. It can be added to taste. Serve with bacon fryings or butter.

1932, Mrs. Nannie Lowery Hitchens (Oklahoma Cherokee)

DOGHEADS DI-GA-NU-LI
Grit roasting ear corn after it gets too hard for roasting ears. It's meal will be as hard as soft mush. Get wide fodder; wash clean and put about 2 or 3 large cooking spoons of this into a leaf of fodder. Have dough about 5 or 6 inches long and as thick as you can wrap up nicely with one long leaf. Put it on the widest end; double back over bread 5 or 6 inches, then around until it will hold the dough; tie and put into kettle of boiling water. Boil until done. Unwrap and eat for bread while hot.

1932, Bess Schrimsher Lewis (Oklahoma Cherokee)

BROADSORED
Hull or shell green beans. Boil until done and add to the above dough and cook the same way. This makes another bread.

1932, Bess Schrimsher Lewis (Oklahoma Cherokee)

ROASTING EAR BREAD
Grate the corn from the cob on a grater, mix amount needed as making corn bread.

1932, Lilah D. Lindsey (Creek)

HOMEMADE CORN GRITTER
Homemade gritters were often made by punching many holes in a piece of tin with a nail. The tin was then fastened to a base of wood with the rough side up (See illus. below)

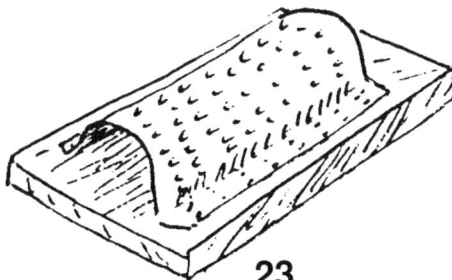

23

GRITTED BREAD

Pick corn when just past the roasting ear stage. Grit corn on a homemade gritter (see pg. 23), and make into bean bread or plain bread. The plain bread, if baked very done, will last a whole week in any weather without souring. This bread can be baked in the woods by spreading leaves of the cucumber tree (*Magnolia acuminata) on a clean spot of ground or on a smooth stone, putting the dough on the leaves and covering with more leaves, and then covering all with live coals and hot ashes and cooking until done.

1950, Mollie Runningwolfe Sequoyah (Cherokee, N.C.)

GRITTED BREAD

Pick the corn just past the roasting ear stage and grit the raw corn on a metal gritter. Add a little lye or soda, and salt. Bake or make into bean bread. Usually, liquid does not have to be added because the natural milk is still in the corn.

1950, Mrs. Clifford Hornbuckle (Cherokee, N.C.)

CORN-DODGER CRACKLING BREAD

Sift corn meal, add pinch of salt, pour in boiling water and make stiff. By using hands make into a ball and mash flat. Bake in real hot oven. Crackling bread is made by adding cracklings to suit taste.

1932, Mrs. S. R. Lewis (Oklahoma Cherokee)

CRACKLING' BREAD

Fry cracklin's to a crisp and grind or mash them. Scald a desired amount of meal, add cracklin's to this. Salt to taste, bake in a hot oven about 10 minutes.

1932, Nannie Lowery Hitchens (Oklahoma Cherokee)

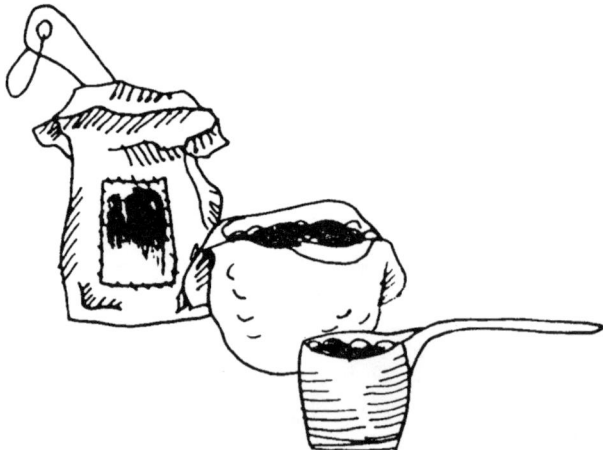

INDIAN SHUCK BREAD
4 or 5 cups of corn meal
3 cups boiling water
1 teaspoon soda
Scald meal and make into cakes rolled into corn shucks. Drop into rapidly boiling water and boil for 10 minutes.

1955, Alice McCurtain Scott, Choctaw
(Daughter of Governor Green McCurtain, the
last elected Governor of the Choctaw tribe.)

PECAN CORN BREAD
Make corn bread in usual manner and stir in 1 cup of pecan meats. Pour into hot greased pan and bake 30 minutes.

1932, Victoria Martin Rogers (Oklahoma Cherokee)

SWEET POTATO BREAD
This bread is made by boiling sweet potatoes, then mixing with corn meal, seasoned with salt and baking powder, if desired, and baking in a hot oven.

1932, Minnie McKee Crowder (Oklahoma Cherokee)

BANAHA (Oklahoma, Cherokee)
Put 1/2 gallon of hominy in warm water. Soak over night, drain and beat into meal, leaving a part of it coarse like grits. Take the grits and make into a gruel and pour boiling water over the meal. Add cooked beans and bean ashes* to make a stiff dough. Make into a roll, wrap in boiled corn shucks and tie in the middle. Boil 4 hours.
*See Bean Ash Cake recipe (see pg. 32)

1955, Mr. & Mrs. William Short (Chickasaw)

PALUSHKA HOWASHKO (Sour Bread)
Made like Banaha (above) except that dough is thinner and beans and bean ashes are omitted. Let the mixture stand until slightly fermented; then bake like corn bread.

1955, Mr. & Mrs. William Short (Chickasaw)

ASH CAKES

Mix cornmeal and warm water into a stiff dough. Rake ashes back from the hot stone at the bottom of fireplace and cover with oak leaves. Place the cornpone on the leaves, cover with more leaves and cover it all with red-hot ashes. Remove pone when done.

1950, Aggie Ross Lossiah (Cherokee, N.C.)

INDIAN CRACKLING CORN PONE

Take 2 parts corn meal to one part cracklings. Salt to taste. Mix well. Pour boiling water over the mixture until it can be formed with the hands. Form into thin cakes and bake. The Indians baked this in out door ovens or on top of the fire.

1955, Virginia Algonquian Apan

CORN BREAD BAKED ON BARK

Cherokees did not carry cooking utensils when traveling, so when it was time to cook bread, the dough was spread on the inside of pieces of bark from the chestnut tree. The bark was stood up before the fire to bake and the combination of wood smoke, bark and hunger made this bread the best any Indian ever ate.

1950, Aggie Ross Lossiah (Cherokee, N.C.)

FRIED CORN BREAD WITH CREAM SAUCE

Slice cold corn bread 1 inch thick and brown in hot grease, place on a dish.
SAUCE: Take equal parts of meat fryings and butter, add 1 tablespoon of flour and brown. Pour in 1 pint of sweet milk; boil until thick. Add cream, salt and pepper to taste. Pour over corn bread and serve hot.

1932, Victoria Martin Rogers (Oklahoma Cherokee)

LOAF BREAD

Scrape green corn from cob, beat into paste, add salt and pepper, shape into rolls 4" X 1 1/2". Wrap rolls in corn husks, drop into boiling water and cook about 45 minutes. This is an early Tamale and may be steamed instead of boiled. Spread with butter when done.

(Iroquois)

INDIAN CORN BREAD

To 1 quart of meal add boiling water. Roll into a loaf and bake slowly for 1 hour.

1932, Mary Jackson Smith (Oklahoma Cherokee)

RAISED CORN BREAD

Take about 4 cups corn meal, sift and stir in luke warm water until a stiff dough is formed. Leave it in the bowl in a warm place to rise. This takes from a day to a day and a half. When it has risen, break it up, add soda, salt, 2 tablespoons sugar, and 1 egg. If dough is too stiff, add buttermilk to soften. Put in greased baking pans, let rise again and bake.

1955, Watie Pettit (Oklahoma Cherokee)

INDIAN CORN LIGHT BREAD

3 pints rye meal	2 cakes yeast
2 tablespoons salt	1 teaspoon soda
3 pints yellow corn meal	1 cup thick molasses
3 tablespoons shortening	

Dissolve yeast in 1/2 cup warm water, scald the meal with 1 pint hot water and let cool. When luke warm add all the remaining ingredients and let rise until double in bulk. Knead and form into loaves. It is much nicer baked in individual pans. Let rise 2 hours and bake at 450 degrees for 15 minutes, then 350 degrees for 30 minutes, making a total of 45 minutes baking time.

1955, Watie Pettit (Oklahoma Cherokee)

SQUAW BREAD

1 pint sweet milk   2 tablespoons baking powder
1 teaspoon salt   1 tablespoon shortening

Use enough flour to make a dough, easily handled, knead and roll out to any desired thickness, cut in pieces, cut 2 slits and cook in kettle of deep fat. Serve with syrup and crisp bacon.

1955, Mr. & Mrs. William Short (Chickasaw)

TAMALES

Mix 1 1/2 cup cornmeal with I 1/2 cup beanmeal, add 2 cups warm water, 1 cup lard or shortening and 1 teaspoon salt. Mix meal and water together. Let stand 20 minutes. Beat lard and salt together until fluffy, then beat in meal mixture until well combined. Measure 2 tablespoons dough into a cornhusk, spread to a 3" x 5" rectangle. Spoon 1 scant tablespoon chopped meat and pepper sauce onto dough. Roll dough up jellyroll fashion. Fold cornhusk over tightly, fold ends in and tie with narrow strips of cornhusk or string. Steam over boiling water, covered, for 40 to 45 minutes. Yield: about 25.
Many Indians used the meat from roasted bird, such as quail or wild turkey in their tamales.

Southwestern and Mexican Indians.

TORTILLA

Combine 2 cups very fine cornmeal with 1 cup water. Mix with hands until dough is moist but holds its shape. Add more water if necessary. Let stand 15 minutes. Divide dough into 12 balls. Dampen dough slightly with water, then roll dough between 2 sheets of waxed paper into a 6" round. Peel top paper off and place tortilla with other paper side up on a hot ungreased griddle, then peel other paper off. Cook about 30 seconds or until edges begin to dry, then turn and cook until surface appears puffy. Repeat with remaining dough. Stack to keep warm. Southwestern and Mexican Indians dipped the tortilla into a hot pepper sauce before eating but today there are many popular fillings for tortillas.

MISCELLANEOUS

TANFULA (Tanfula--hominy)
(To be eaten fresh)
Take any amount of hominy grits or prepared Tanfula (4 cups makes quite a lot). Use cold water to cover. Cook over low heat for about 4 hours or longer. Add a pinch of soda in the Tanfula as it starts cooking. When the Tanfula starts getting done it will stick if not stirred often.

1955, Alice McCurtain Scott (Choctaw)

SOUR TANFULA
Use any amount of hominy grits or prepared Tanfula and cold water to cover. Cook over a slow fire 4 hours or longer until done. Take a handful of clean wood ashes (some Indians say ashes from a black jack tree are best), put in an iron skillet (the lye in the ashes will eat any other kind of vessel), pour 1 cup of boiling water over the ashes, let settle, then strain. Use 2 or 3 tablespoons of the lye water for each gallon of Tanfula. Do not put this lye water in until the Tanfula is nearly done as it will make it mushy if put in too soon. Some Indians used more of this "ash water" in their Tanfula, but use it sparingly as it is lye. Tanfula made in this way can be put in a crock to sour. This lye will tend to thicken the Tanfula so boil some water and pour over the Tanfula in the crock. It will take perhaps 3 days for this to sour. Tanfula made this way will sour, but it will not rot. If made with soda it cannot be soured, but it will rot.

1955, Alice McCurtain Scott (Choctaw)

REMEDIES USING CORN
Eat parched corn for long wind.

Make tea from the yellow strands of silk beneath the husk of corn for a diuretic and for gravel.

Boil bark of the Basswood tree (Linden) and stir cornmeal into the resulting ooze to make a poultice for boils.

Eat parched corn to treat jaundice.

These remedies are offered for you interest only and must not be used as substitutes for professional medical attention for any serious health disturbance or for any chronic warning symptoms. When in doubt consult a physician.

WAH-WE-NO-KONE-MIN-GUY

Gather green corn when too hard for roasting ears and grate. (The Indians used the jaw of deer, grating on the teeth). Place the grated corn in the sun to dry. Cook and serve like rice or oatmeal or can be used in bread.

1932, Lena Barnard (Piankasaw)

PARCHED CORN

Parch corn in hot ashes until brown. Sift ashes out of corn and beat until a grit stage is reached. Sift meal until nothing but the grits are left, add grits to hot water to make a soup to suit your taste. Hunters often carried parched meal on long trips instead of rations. It made a very filling food, as about a handful is enough for a meal.

1955, Watie Pettit (Oklahoma Cherokee)

CORNSHUCK DOLLS

Dried cornshucks from the mature ear of corn were often used to make dolls. The art of "Cornshuck-Doll-Making" reached a high level of artistry, with dolls bearing the likeness of the Indian people both in facial characteristics and in clothing types, styles & colors. Cornshuck dolls can still be found in many homes and are sold in some craft shops.

HOW - TO'S

DRYING CORN FOR FRESHNESS

The corn, flint corn in preference, to be plucked when soft and ready for roasting ears. The outer husks to be taken off, and the corn to be boiled thorougly. The inner husks, after this, are to be drawn back so as to enable it to be tied up in bunches. Under a scaffolding raised on poles, it is then to be suspended over a slow fire, till it becomes perfectly dry and rather smoked. It may be some days in undergoing this preparation. When thorougly dry, it must be removed, and hung in a dry place so as not to mould. When wanted for use, the grains must be shelled and boiled over again. At first it will be found shrunken and as hard as stone, but cooking will bring it out fresh and soft.

1830's, Mrs. John Ross, collected by J.H. Payne.
(Mrs. Ross was the wife of the Principal Chief of the
Cherokee Nation at the time of the Removal of the I830's.)

RECIPE FOR DRIED CORN

Boil corn on cob in clean water. Cut from cob to drying board; let it remain in the sun until thoroughly dried.

1932, Roberta Campbell Lawson (Delaware)

DRYING CORN

Cut top 3/4 of kernels off cob of roasting ears. Spread fresh uncooked corn on cheese cloth stretched on a frame and put in sun to dry. Turn corn about 4 times a day and dry until all juice has been evaporated and kernels have become very hard. Store in a bag or a covered earthen jar in a dry place. To cook dried corn, take as much as you desire to serve, cover with an inch of water, salt to taste, season with any meat seasoning and cook until done. This is delicious with fresh pork dishes. Dried corn will keep indefinitely.

1955, Mr. Watie Pettit (Oklahoma Cherokee)

SHAWNEE RECIPE FOR DRYING CORN

Select corn that is firm but not hard. Scrape off of cob into deep pan. When pan is full, set in slow oven and bake until thoroughly heated through, an hour or more. Remove from oven and turn pone out to cool. Later crumble on drying board in the sun and when thoroughly dried, sack for winter.

1932, Roberta Campbell Lawson (Delaware)

DRIED CORN

Take good roasting ears, cut from the cob and spread on a clean sheet in the hot sun 2 or 3 days until thoroughly dry. Put in sacks and hang up. It is then ready the year around and fine for winter. Cook like canned corn.

1932, Lilan D. Lindsey (Creek)

CURING THE CORN LEAVES

Gather even, broad, mature leaf blades from the corn plants. Bunch the pointed ends together and tie, hanging in the shade to dry. Dip in hot water before using.

1950, Aggie Ross Lossiah (Cherokee, N.C.)

BEAN ASH CAKES (Indian Soda)

Put bean hulls in a big pot. Burn until they become ashes. Mix with water, make into small cakes about 3" in circumference, and dry in the sun. They are then ready for use.

1955, Mr. & Mrs. William Short (Chickasaw)

LYE

In all instances where lye is mentioned, the water dripped from wood ashes is intended. Any wood may be used; however, the black jack wood when burned to ashes makes the strongest lye. The ashes are placed in a vessel with a perforated bottom, pour hot water over and let drain until all strength is exhausted.

1932, Lilah D. Lindsey (Creek)

ASH LYE

Burn black jack wood to ashes. Place in cloth sack and pour boiling water through ashes draining water into a pan.

1955, Mr. Watie Pettit (Oklahoma Cherokee)